100
TIPS FOR A STRESS-FREE WEDDING MORNING

HELEN TOZER

100 Tips For A Stress-Free Wedding Morning
Copyright © Helen Tozer 2010
All rights reserved.

First Published in Great Britain in 2010 by Tozer Media

ISBN 978-0-9564965-3-9

Tozer Media
Station Road
Ilminster
Somerset
TA19 9BG

www.tozer-media.com

No part of this publication may be reproduced, stored in or introduced into a retrieval system, or transmitted, in any form, or by any means (electronic, mechanical, photocopying, recording or otherwise) without the prior written permission of the publisher. All inquiries should be made to the publisher at the address above. This book is sold subject to the condition that it shall not, by way of trade or otherwise, be lent, resold, hired out, or otherwise circulated without the publishers' prior consent in any form of binding or cover other that that in which it is published and without a similar condition including this condition being imposed on the subsequent purchaser. Whilst the author and publisher have made every reasonable effort to ensure this publication is free from error, neither author, publisher nor distributor assume any responsibility for errors, omissions or contrary interpretation of the subject matter herein.

Book design by Chris Tozer
www.christozer.com

Printed and bound in Great Britain

CONTENTS

	Acknowledgements	*5*
	About This Book	*7*
	Introduction	*9*
Chapter 1	A Bride's Guide	*11*
Chapter 2	The Wedding Dress	*15*
Chapter 3	The Bridesmaids	*18*
Chapter 4	The Day Before	*21*
Chapter 5	A Calm Environment	*23*
Chapter 6	How to Relax	*24*
Chapter 7	Hair Tips	*29*
Chapter 8	Make-Up Tips	*32*
Chapter 9	General Advice	*37*
Chapter 10	A Guide to Timings	*40*
Chapter 11	Top Ten Wedding Tips	*44*
Chapter 12	Helen's Hair Portfolio	*46*
	Internet Resources	*48*
	About The Author	*53*
	Notes	*55*

ACKNOWLEDGEMENTS

I would like to thank everyone who has helped me to produce '100 Tips For A Stress-Free Wedding Morning'.

Grateful thanks go to Vanessa Mason of 'You & Your Wedding' magazine for the use of her image, along with Jessica Potter and all the other brides who allowed me to use their images and encouraged me to write the book.

Special thanks to my daughter Lucy for sorting my notes, and providing the make-up tips; my son Chris for designing the book and to my husband Peter for editing and publishing.

ABOUT THIS BOOK

I'm fortunate that I have had the privilege to be part of, and share in, over 150 wedding day preparations. My occupation as a bridal hairdresser has given me plenty of wedding morning experience. I've seen so often that it's this part of the planning process that seems to get less attention than the rest.

I've observed frantic situations where little things had been overlooked or forgotten which then puts a damper on the whole day's enjoyment. Luckily, my familiarity with the necessary procedures has allowed me to solve a few problems and soothe a few nerves on more than one occasion.

Because I was able to provide the answers to queries and solve some urgent problems on the day, several of my clients suggested I should write a book of tips and hints. They pointed out that there were dozens of wedding planning articles in magazines, on the internet and in books dealing with the build-up to the day, but nothing about the wedding morning in particular.

So one cold and snow-covered morning in January when it was quiet, and the weather outside stopped me from going anywhere, I started to jot down a few notes.
I assembled a collection of handy tips and lists for quick reference. I'm sure that you'll find the result helpful and easy to use. Just what you need when you're under a bit of pressure.

I thoroughly enjoy my profession and I'm passionate about providing a perfect, dedicated and enjoyable experience for my brides. I sincerely hope this book will help you to sail serenely through your wedding morning. With my warmest best wishes to you for an exciting and wonderful day.

INTRODUCTION

It's the most exciting day of your life, full of excitement, happiness and joy. For months beforehand it will be the main thing on your mind, the main topic of conversation and your full attention will be focussed on this one glorious occasion. Not so long ago it was the bride's mother that did all the planning and organising. Nowadays it's more likely to be you!

As your wedding day draws closer the anticipation and excitement starts to increase – and before you know it, it's the morning of the wedding. This is when you discover that maybe you are not as cool, calm and collected as you thought you would be!

The chances are that you'll sleep lightly the night before with everything churning around in your mind. You're determined to enjoy every minute of the day – and so you should, it's a fantastic feeling.

But when it comes to the actual wedding morning, for many families, everything seems to dissolve into chaos. No one seems to know what to do or the correct sequence of events. Probably the biggest mistake everyone makes is to leave it too late to get ready and fail to appreciate just how fast time flies on the morning.

The purpose of '100 Tips For A Stress-Free Wedding' is to highlight the more important details and some of the little (but nonetheless significant) things that often get overlooked or forgotten. The aim is to make sure that every aspect of your wedding day morning is covered.

The tips you are about to discover are based on my practical experience. They're intended to ensure that this - your most important day - proceeds calmly and smoothly.

Chapter One
A BRIDE'S GUIDE

The single most important secret to a successful and stress-free day is to surround yourself with competent and caring attendants. Always engage professional hair and beauty artists and appoint bridesmaids that are supportive, obliging & committed.

Tempting as it may be, try not to do everything yourself.

Get some family members and friends to ease some of the pressure; delegate jobs to others. They will love to help and it makes them feel good that they have played a part in your special day.

Your wedding morning experience should be relaxed and calm, dedicated to your preparation; your hair, your make-up and getting dressed.

BEFORE THE DAY

01 Try on your wedding shoes several times before the wedding day to make sure that they are comfortable and don't rub anywhere.

02 Think about your heels and how increasing your height will compare with the height of your husband-to-be. You will not want to tower over him on the day!

03 Decide where to have your hair done on the morning; at home or in a salon. For a stress free morning I recommend that you have the hairdresser and make-up artist come to you.

04 Once you have chosen your underwear, try it on with the dress to make sure no straps are visible.

ON THE DAY

05 Make sure that you have included the make-up you will need for the morning after the wedding in your overnight bag.

06 Try not to wear a bra or any tight fitting tops in the morning – you will want to avoid strap marks on your skin.

07 Put your engagement ring on your right hand and remove any jewellery that you normally wear e.g. a watch or bracelet.

08 Pack your camera and charger – don't forget to charge it up the night before.

09 Keep some Imodium in the house just in case you are really nervous and get caught short!

10 *Delegate someone to take care of your bag of essentials for the day*

- Nail file
- Face powder
- Lipstick
- Small sewing kit
- Safety pins
- Grips and comb
- Small can of hairspray
- Tampons (if needed)
- Small mirror
- Breath freshener/Mints
- Paracetamol/Ibuprofen
- Perfume

11 *Dedicate a specific table or sideboard to place everything you need to get ready*

Doing so will avoid rushing around to find important items. For example:

- Underwear
- Garter
- Stockings/hold ups
- Perfume
- Jewellery (Necklace, Earrings, Tiara)
- Lipstick
- Hair grips
- Tiara
- Hair and Make-up trial photos
- Camera
- Deodorant
- Silk Flowers
- Payment for hair/make-up artist/florist
- Bridesmaid's gifts
- Something old/new/borrowed/blue

And of course, allocate another area for larger items:

- The dress
- Shoes
- Veil
- Umbrella
- Shawl (if cold weather)

THE WEDDING DRESS
Chapter Two

When you go for your dress fitting make sure to take your appointed helper for the wedding day; be it your bridesmaid or a family member. They will need to see how you are expected to get into the dress and fasten it, particularly if it's a lace-up.

12 Try on your new underwear before the wedding day to make sure it doesn't rub or feel odd in any way. Putting on new underwear is always lovely, but it can also be uncomfortable.

13 Buttons/Laces/Zip? Make sure that whoever is dressing you on the day does not have painted nails; a red or coloured nail polish can rub off onto the dress.

14 If your dressing assistant does not have painted nails then at least make sure their nails are tidy and filed smooth to avoid any hitches.

15 Insist that anyone who is allowed to touch the Bride's dress must make sure that their hands are washed and clean so as not to leave any grubby marks.

16 If you have to put your dress on over your head then use a pillowcase to cover your hair and face. This will make sure that your hair stays in place and your make-up doesn't smudge onto the dress.

STOCKINGS OR TIGHTS?

17 Stockings are so romantic but if you are not used to wearing suspenders you should try them on before the wedding day. They can be tricky to fasten and some find them quite awkward to wear. They do take a bit of getting used to.

18 Tights can be too warm so hold-ups can be a cooler option.

19 Always put your shoes on after your dress to avoid hitching or catching it.

20 *Whether tights or hold-ups, try them on with your shoes. You may find them slippery in your new shoes so consider some gel inserts for your heels or insoles*

THE VEIL

21 Remember to take your veil out of its wrapper and hang it up the night before. If it is creased, hang it up in the bathroom so that the steam can help the creases to fall out

TOP TIPS

22 A veil is usually attached to a comb which is inserted into your hair. To be doubly sure that the veil stays in place, ask your hairdresser to secure the comb with hair grips.

23 Remember to make sure that you visit the toilet before dressing: it's not so easy once you're dressed. This applies to the Bridesmaids too.

24 Make sure that, if you use a roll on deodorant, you apply it in plenty of time before you get dressed to allow it to dry.

THE BRIDESMAIDS
Chapter Three

It's not always an easy decision to make, but you must choose your bridesmaids carefully. It's a privilege to be chosen as a bridesmaid and their task is to support and help you. After all, it is your special day and you are the centre of attention – not them! They need to be reliable and willing to help over the months approaching the wedding day. You are going to need their help with all the planning and preparation.

If you decide not to have any bridesmaids then you can ask close friends or family members to help with some of the tasks. This way you can cut costs and they will feel involved and appreciated at the same time.
Think about your flower girl having a wrist corsage rather than a bouquet. This will save her having to hold it, while at the same time trying to help you.

On the morning of the wedding it will be the chief bridesmaid's responsibility, not yours, to sort out any problems that arise.

25 Your chief bridesmaid will be responsible for organising your hen night as well as advising you and giving you moral support. Her role starts as soon as she has been invited to assist you. She will be expected to ensure that the other bridesmaids, flower girls and page boys know what to do on the day.

26 If your Bridesmaids are doing their own make-up and hair make sure that you will be happy with the result. If you think that they may not be able to get the presentation just right, suggest or even offer to get it done professionally.

27 When you arrive at the church she will arrange your dress and veil for you. She will also make sure that you are calm and ready to walk down the aisle – choose her carefully!

28 She will also be looking after your bag of essentials which will include your emergency kit, so she is a very important aide!

BRIDESMAID TOP TIP

29 *Ensure that your chief bridesmaid has all the important telephone numbers on her mobile phone:*

- the florist
- the venue
- the hairdresser
- the make-up artist
- your Mother
- your husband-to-be
- and of course, yours!

Chapter Four
THE DAY BEFORE

Now is the time to start relaxing a little because all of your preparation and planning is about to unfold.

30 Get all of your ironing done today. Hang it up, all ready to go on the day. The last thing you want to be doing on your wedding day is ironing. Make sure everyone in the immediate wedding party gets their ironing out of the way too.

31 Don't forget to remove the labels that may be stuck onto the soles of your new shoes.

32 Remember to pack your overnight bag with toiletries ready for the next day.

33 Have a manicure and pedicure the day before. This will allow the polish to cure hard. Of course, you won't be able to do anything afterwards that may chip your nails.

34 Have all cheques or cash ready in envelopes to pay people on the day i.e. hairdresser, make-up artist, florist.

35 Try to avoid eating spicy foods laced with garlic the day before. You'll be greeting and talking to a lot of people.

36 If not already taken care of, organise someone to look after your pets. Maybe a trusted friend or neighbour could do this for you.

37 Cut off all tags & labels from your jewellery, dresses and underwear that you will be wearing on the day.

Doing it now avoids everyone hunting for a pair of scissors on the day

Now relax, enjoy a small drink and try to get as much rest and sleep as you can. Tomorrow is going to be a long day!

A CALM ENVIRONMENT
Chapter Five

The wedding morning preparation is a big part of your experience. It should be a happy time full of laughter and anticipation but in a calm and relaxed atmosphere. You do not need a last minute rush to unsettle you. Try to leave the house feeling ready and calm, not rushed or stressed.

I know this may seem repetitive but I believe this is probably the most important tip of all: relax and enjoy every precious moment of one of the most enjoyable and memorable days of your life. If you enjoy yourself, then your guests will also.

38 On the morning of your wedding surround yourself with calm people. Their relaxed state will transfer to others and contribute to everyone enjoying the day with you.

39 Limit the number of people helping you on the morning. You will not appreciate lots of people getting in the way or hanging around with nothing to do.

40 Make sure that other members of the wedding party are dressed and ready before you; then if you need help, they are available to assist.

Chapter Six
HOW TO RELAX

On the day of your wedding trying to relax will be one of your main concerns. It's not an easy state to master, considering the circumstances. The subconscious worry about everything going to plan; the weather; relatives getting on; being late and walking down the aisle with everyone's gaze fixed on you - all leads to tension. It can sometimes leave a bride stressed.

My role as a wedding hair stylist is to make my brides look beautiful and feel fantastic on the day. However, within months of starting my service, I soon realised that I could also benefit my clients by helping to calm them and prepare them for the forthcoming nervous tensions of the day. I now see it as part of the service I provide, while deriving great satisfaction from doing my bit to help.

Over time, I have discovered a few tips and tricks to help calm nerves and reduce tension. These little tips can benefit everyone in the wedding party, including the Bride and Groom. They can be applied at any other time too, whenever nervous tension or pressure prevents us from performing well or enjoying an event.

I will never forget how I was so nervous on my own wedding day that it prevented me from enjoying it as much as I could. Before I knew it, the day was over and I had done all that worrying for nothing! Have a look at the following suggestions and pick a relaxation technique that works best for you.

MAKE A LIST OF THINGS TO DO

41 Do away with the stress of trying to remember what you need to do. Listing things in order of importance or urgency helps reduce tension. That way you tick off the list, safe in the knowledge that nothing has been forgotten.

TRY A LITTLE YOGA

42 Sit up straight in your chair and let your arms drop limp at your sides. Breathe in, and as you breathe out, lean forward and rest your chest on your thighs. Remain there for five seconds, then slowly sit up and breathe in again. Repeat this action three or four times until you feel calmer.

ASSOCIATE A PLEASANT MEMORY

43 Look at some photos or touch an object that brings you pleasant memories. It can be an item from your childhood, a piece of your grandmother's jewellery or a lucky charm.

CALMING REMEDIES

46 Several of the Brides that I have given support to tell me that they found it helpful to carry a small dropper bottle of Rescue Remedy with them. It may be that you don't have much faith in this, but many brides seem to feel much better after a dose; believing that it works wonders. In an uptight situation, anything that calms the mind is essential. Rescue Remedy is readily available at most chemists, health food stores or pharmacies.

VISUALISATION

44 This can work for some people but you need to be in a quiet place, not in the middle of all the action!

- Close your eyes.
- Gently take in and release two deep breaths.
- Now think of your favorite place in the whole world.
- Now take yourself there.
- See what you're doing.
- Hear the sounds that surround you.
- Smell the air.
- Feel the textures around you.
- Stay in your special place for a minute or two, then take two deep breaths.
- Allow yourself to come back to the present, and open your eyes.

RELAX WITH AN ESSENCE

45 Apply a little lavender or mint oil on your inner wrist and take a whiff every so often. Lavender can be relaxing, while mint is invigorating.

HYPNOSIS

47 Consider having hypnosis before the day or practice self-hypnosis. There are several good books on the subject.

PICTURE AIR AS A CLOUD

48 The following technique has become my favourite way of reducing tension. One of my brides told me about it; she said that it works for her every time. I've tried it myself and it works for me too. It's so simple.

Close your eyes open up your imagination and focus on your breathing. Breathe in and out deeply and gently. As your breathing becomes calm and regular, imagine that the air comes to you as a fluffy cloud. It fills you and goes out again. If you wish, imagine the cloud to be a particular colour.

• • •

If none of these things help you then try to turn your thoughts away from nervousness to excitement. Think about all the happy moments you'll soon be spending with your new husband. Above all else, if you can start and end your day laughing you will have found one of the secrets to stress and tension relief.

Chapter Seven
HAIR TIPS

If possible try to arrange it that your hairdresser and make-up artist come to you for the wedding morning preparation. To do so will save you the stress and worry of traffic hold-ups getting to the salon and if the weather is wet and windy, you won't run the risk of spoiling everything. If you have chosen your hair and beauty team carefully they will be professionals and work together as a team to get you ready in good time. They should carry out their duties calmly and confidently which in turn will help you and your family to feel calm and relaxed.

49** **Have the photographs from your hair trial printed and ready for your stylist. Both of you will then be certain about the agreed style

50 Invest in a good quality shampoo to suit your hair type and make sure to rinse thoroughly afterwards.

51 Your scalp produces natural oils so when you add a conditioner to your roots, they become greasy. Your hairstyle will hold better if you apply conditioner only to the ends of your hair.

52 If you have fine or thin hair, consider using clip on extensions to add volume and length if required. They are inexpensive and can look very natural.

53 Wash your hair the day before your wedding or early in the morning of the wedding day. It is important that your hair is clean and dry for the hairdresser to style.

54 If you are growing your hair long for your wedding day, make sure to have regular trims from your hairdresser, without cutting too much off. A trim six weeks before your wedding is perfect. I have known girls to have long hair at their trial, only to find that their hairdresser has been scissor happy and left it short. Then the trial style can't be achieved – disaster!

55 If your choice is for cascading curls on your wedding day, and you have thick, long, single length hair, it won't hold well without layers being applied to it.

56 If there are several heads of hair to be styled on the morning, make sure you get yours done early on. Be guided by your hairstylist of course; just make sure that you're not the last to be done with time running out!

57 *Avoid silicone based shampoos & conditioners. They will just coat your hair rather than condition it; leaving your hair looking lank and greasy. Check the ingredients when you buy your hair products*

Chapter Eight
MAKE-UP TIPS

Hair or Make-up first? Good question! It will depend on the timing. If you are having curlers, get them completed first then have your make-up applied. After that, back to the hairdresser.

58 Any facial waxing/plucking should be done at least a couple of days before your wedding day. If you leave it too late then you may still have redness or swelling on the big day.

59 Before your make-up artist gets to work, make sure that you have cleaned your teeth, blown your nose and put in your contact lenses, if you wear them. If you need to apply eye drops or false teeth do it before putting on your make up.

60 Always make sure that you have removed any previous make-up before starting.

61 Try not to blow your nose after the make-up has been applied. If you do, you may remove some of the foundation and expose a red nose!

62 After your make-up has been applied, at any time that you feel tearful remember to gently pat or dab your eyes dry with a clean tissue – don't wipe them dry. Doing so will smudge or wipe off the make-up, and your photos will not look good.

63 Consider water and smudge proof make-up as a must-have. Most make-up counters in stores will have an advisor willing to give you some free samples to try out.

64 Be sure to try out any new foundations or make-up before your wedding day, just in case you react to them

65 More lipstick and other touch-ups can be applied just before you leave for the church.

66 Remember that you will be able to refer to the trial photo's to get your wedding day 'look' just right.

67 Take advice from your make-up artist and always buy a lipstick and face powder that you are both happy with.

68 Ask your chief bridesmaid to look after your lipstick/lip gloss so that you can re-apply or touch-up throughout the day as you eat and drink.

APPLYING YOUR OWN MAKE-UP

Apply your make-up in such a way that you still look like you; just enough to enhance and emphasise your features, but still keep it natural. You want people to recognise you!

69 Use a foundation that is a really good colour match. Using one that is too dark for your skin can make you look 'orange' with a foundation mark on your jaw line.

70 If you suffer with red cheeks or a red nose, use a 'green stick' on the red area before applying your foundation. It will counteract the redness and give you a clear complexion.

71 If your eyebrows are lighter than your hair colour use a slightly darker eye shadow on your eyebrows, in place of eyebrow pencil. This will give a much softer look while framing your eyes.

72 *Don't use eyeliner on the inside of your eye-line if you have small eyes. To do so will make them look even smaller*

73 *Use an eyelash curler before applying mascara; this will give the appearance of longer and thicker eye lashes*

74 When using dark eye shadow use it in the corners of your eyes and in your socket line. This will give the effect of a larger/wider eye and flatter your bone structure.

75 If you are not used to wearing lipstick, use a colour that is flattering and fairly natural with just a little colour, or maybe a gloss. You will feel more comfortable and still look special.

Chapter Nine
GENERAL ADVICE

Remember, that I have written this guide to act as a quick, ready reference of essential tips; to help improve the morning's activity flow, reduce your stress and ease the worry about your wedding morning preparations.

Some of the things that needed to be considered didn't warrant a chapter or category of their own, so I thought it best to have section of general tips for you to dip into. Have a quick look and perhaps make your own notes to refer to.

76 Don't be tempted to have a few too many drinks the night before with your family or friends. The last thing you want is a hangover on your wedding day. Save it all for the big day when you get to party!

77 Young Bridesmaids or Flower girls should not arrive for preparation too early. They can quickly and easily become bored waiting, particularly if there are several of them. You will not want the distraction of boisterous kiddies' running around while you get ready.

78 Remember to organise someone to take care of your house security. Make sure that all lights are switched off and all windows and doors are locked.

79 If you are decorating the venue, draw a diagram of the table layout with a seating plan. Delegate a close friend or bridesmaid to be in charge of this task.

FLOWERS AND BUTTONHOLES

80 Some buttonholes can be too heavy for delicate or lightweight tops and dresses. They can flop forward and pull on the fabric, distorting it and then your photos don't look so good. Talk to your florist about silk flowers maybe, or use magnets to fasten them. You may even decide to attach your flowers to your handbag or wrist.

81 Your florist should be able to give you advice about the church flowers and after the ceremony will transfer them to the reception venue. Make sure to ask them to prepare the table decorations and any gift bouquets for the reception. These are usually presented during the groom's speech.

82 Delegate the collection of bouquets, corsages and buttonholes from the florist. Have a list of items drawn up; whoever has the task ticks off a check list so nothing gets forgotten.

83 Remember, the Ladies corsage is always placed on the right.

84 Gentlemen's buttonholes are always on the left lapel.

DRESSING UP

85 Here's a little job for the Mother in Law: ask the tailor to teach her how to tie cravats on the Groom and the Ushers. She can also be in charge of the buttonholes.

86 If wearing a hat, to avoid 'hat head' back comb the hair after blow drying to give more volume and lift. Finish the style with hair spray and allow to dry. Put the hat on, always at a slight angle. After removing the hat, brush the hair to remove the back-combing and the hair will bounce back into style. Then apply more hair spray to hold.

87 Don't be too anxious about children keeping still while having their hair done. Children love to dress up and are usually willing to have their hair done - as long as it's not their mum doing it!

88 If your Mum or Mum-in-Law are wearing a fascinator instead of a hat, it will be easier to fix it firmly if their hair is back combed. This gives the fascinator comb more body to hold onto, while using grips to keep it in place.

KEEPING COOL AND WARM

89 If the wedding is taking place on a hot summer's day get a mini fan to help to keep you cool. Ask your Dad to keep it in his pocket prior to arriving at the church, and then pass it to your husband or chief bridesmaid to look after it for you.

90 To keep warm on a chilly day think about wearing a shawl before arrival at the church. Keep the bridesmaids warm with a shawl, cardigan or a pashmina for the adult bridesmaids.

Chapter Ten
A GUIDE TO TIMINGS

Being organised and following a timetable on the morning of the wedding is crucial. Time ticks away at a rapid rate, especially in the last hour.

THE WEDDING MORNING TRIAL RUN

91 Make sure to have a trial run of travel to the church a week or few days beforehand. Preferably, choose the same day and time of day as your wedding. For instance, if your wedding is on a Saturday at 1.30 pm then have the trial run on the same day a week beforehand. You may need to factor in local traffic influences such as schools out, factories out or building/road works. This way you can establish your timings to prevent known delays.

92 Remember that the Mother of the bride and the bridesmaids have to leave for the church before the bride.

93 If your Mum and bridesmaids are using the same car as you then it is important to get the timing right, allowing enough time for the driver to get back to collect you and your Dad.

94 Don't forget, that the photographer will want to take photos of your arrival at the church and this can take several minutes. Always allow plenty of time for these activities.

THE MORNING SCHEDULE

95 Set up an early morning rota for the bathroom. Everyone fights for it first thing and you won't want to wait around for any males to finish shaving.

96 Unless you have washed your hair the night before, wash it first thing in the morning; get your hairdresser's advice here. You cannot wash/bath/shower after your hair and make-up has been completed. It may seem an obvious point to make, but it happens!

97 It is important that you have a breakfast. If you feel too nervous or excited, try to snack on some toast or eat some fruit, maybe a banana.

98 Drink or sip plenty of water to avoid getting dehydrated, but not too much, so that you need to keep visiting the toilet.

99 Aim to be ready at least one hour before you need to leave the house. This will then leave you enough time for the finishing touches e.g. fixing buttonholes, attaching your veil, re-applying lipstick, photo session and maybe a celebration drink!

...AND FINALLY

100 When it comes to walking down the aisle, remember that your father is on your left hand side! It's suprising what you can forget if you have not prepared for a calm wedding morning!

WEDDING MORNING TIMETABLE

Depending on the local traffic conditions and the distance from home or hotel to the church, here is an example of a calm and structured morning; for a wedding at 1 pm with the bride, two bridesmaids and mum.

7:00 am Rise and shine. Shower, wash hair, blast dry.

7:15 am Try to have some breakfast; it will set you up for the day.

7:30 am Hairdresser and Make-up artist arrive.
Dedicate the next three hours to hair and make up for the two bridesmaids, your mum and yourself.

10:00 am Mum gets dressed.
Mum might think this is a bit early, but it is the only time that she will have to take care of herself.

10:30 am Bridesmaids get dressed.

10:45 am Bridesmaids gifts from the bride and groom are presented. Father of the bride gets dressed. Photographer arrives.

11:00 am Bride starts to get dressed.
Helped by mum and bridesmaids

11:30 am Everyone ready! Last touches of make-up. Veil attached if worn. Button holes pinned in place. Celebratory drinks. Last photos before leaving for the church.

12:15 pm Photographer leaves for the church.

12:30 pm Mum and bridesmaids leave for the church.

12:45 pm Bride and father leave for the church.

1:00 pm The ceremony.

Chapter Eleven
HELEN'S TOP 10 WEDDING TIPS

It's usually the little things that cause the most tension and worry. These 10 simple tips will contribute to the smooth running of your wedding day. They have been put together as a result of practical experience.

PLAN YOUR HAIR TRIAL WELL IN ADVANCE

01 Arrange your hair and make-up trial between two to six months prior to your wedding. This gives you time to consider a different style, if needs be.

GET PHOTOS ON THE DAY OF THE TRIAL

02 Have photos taken of your chosen hair style and make-up on the day of your trial. You can then refer to the photos on the wedding morning and your hairdresser will know exactly what to do.

DON'T FORGET YOUR BROLLY!

03 Purchase a wedding umbrella. They're normally white and can be used in brilliant sunshine as well as wet weather. You'll now look cool in both situations. For an online source of umbrellas try: www.artumbrellas.co.uk

MAKE SURE THAT YOUR UNDERWEAR IS COMFORTABLE

04 Try your suspenders and stockings before your wedding day to make sure they are comfortable.

MANICURE BEFORE THE WEDDING DAY

05 Have a pedicure and manicure the day before to make sure that the polish is cured and hard.

PLAN YOUR TAN WELL IN ADVANCE

06 If you're planning on a false tan, make sure to have a practice run 3 to 4 weeks beforehand. This way you'll find out in good time if you react to it badly, or it turns out streaky.

MAKE SURE THAT YOU ARE COMFORTABLE WITH YOUR EYELASHES

07 If you are having false eyelashes, practice putting them on and wearing them before the wedding day. You need to know in advance that you will be comfortable with them.

PROTECT YOUR HAIR AND MAKE-UP

08 When getting ready on the morning of the wedding day always wear a zipped or buttoned top, never a pullover. Then, you can take it off without disturbing your hair and make-up.

WAXING AND PLUCKING

09 Make sure to wax and pluck a few days before the wedding day. You want to avoid the possibility of any sore red marks and swellings.

TAKE CARE WITH THE CORSAGE

10 Remember that mum's corsage is always on the right hand side. Don't have it made too big; it will distort fine fabrics and flop forward, which won't look good in the photographs. Ask the florist if they can use magnets to hold the corsage in place or consider lightweight silk flowers as an alternative.

Chapter Twelve
HELEN'S HAIR PORTFOLIO

There are so many different hairstyle choices and not all hairstyles will suit everyone. Your own hairstyle will depend on factors such as age, facial structure and mood preference i.e. glamorous, romantic, modern or classic. Below is just a small selection of some of my bridal hairstyling, completed for hair trials and actual weddings.

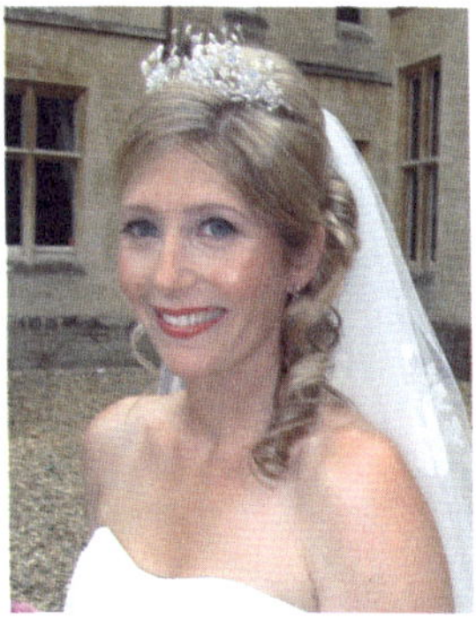
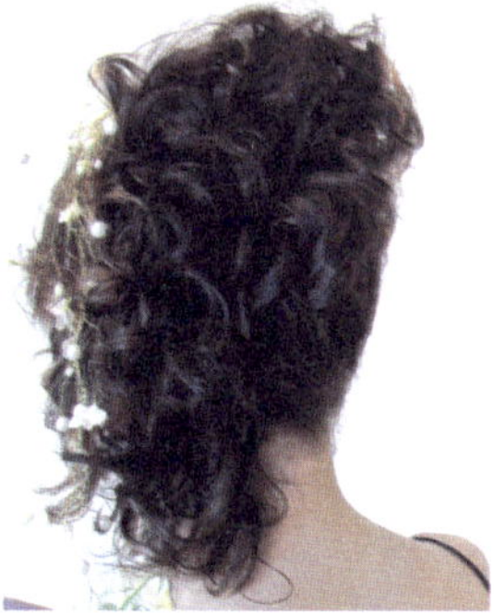
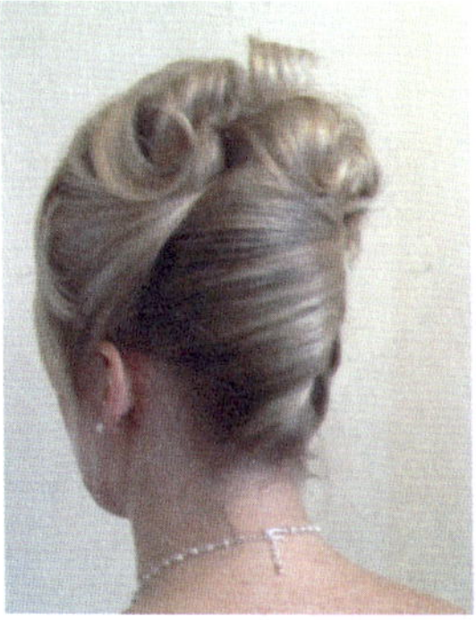
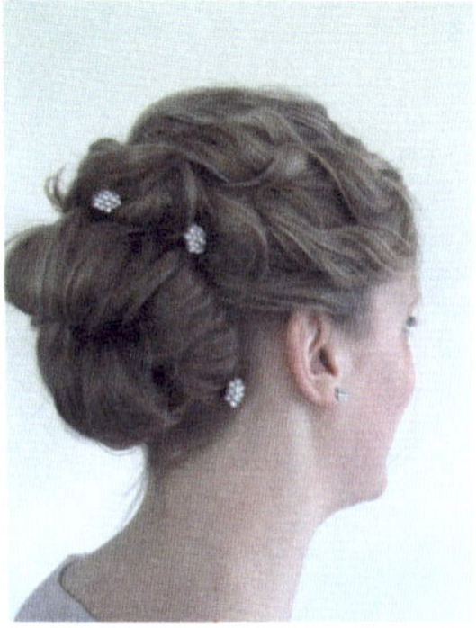
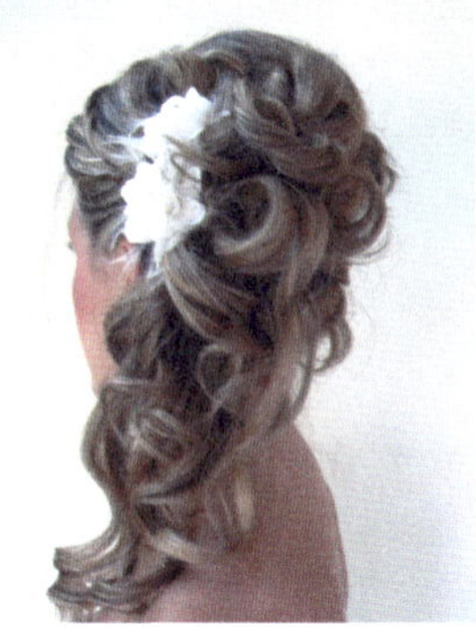
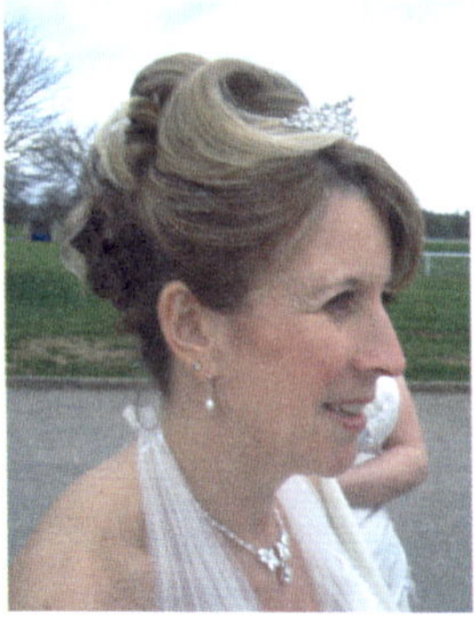
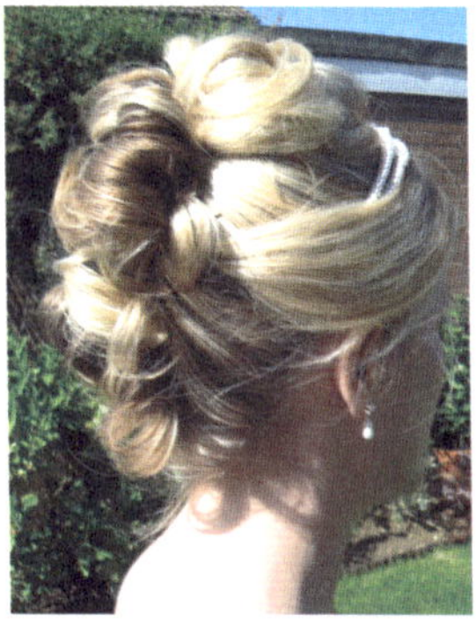
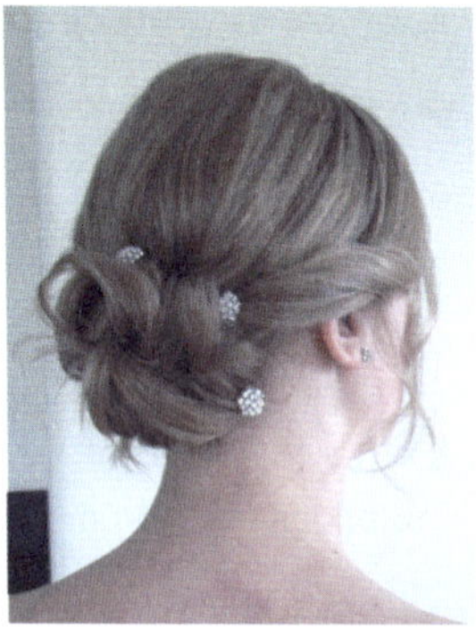
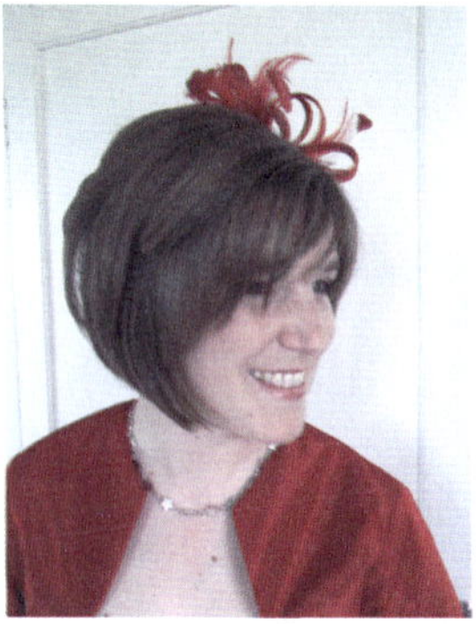
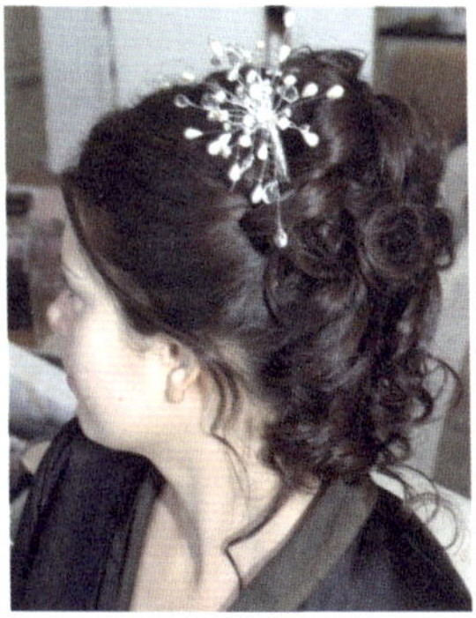
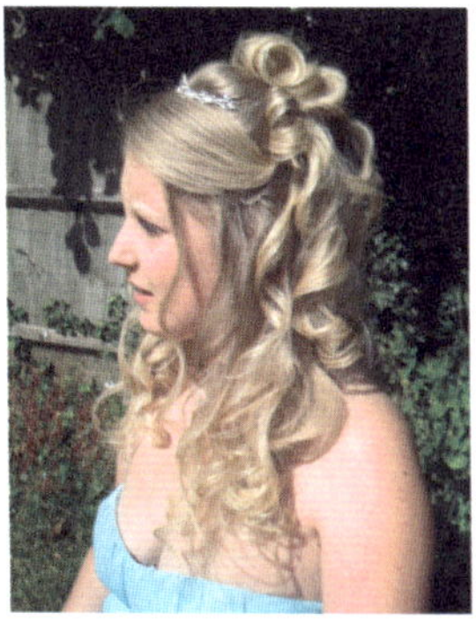
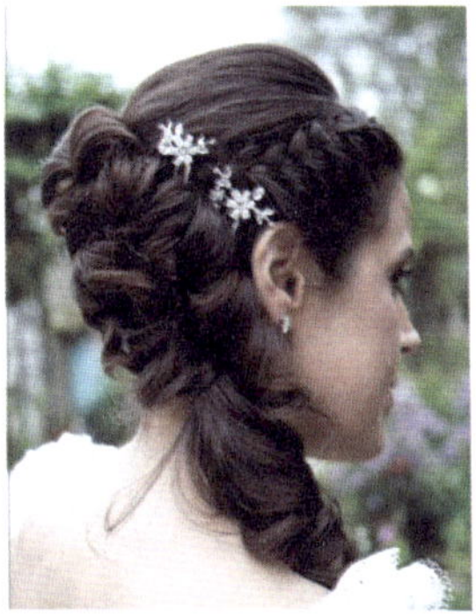

Appendix
INTERNET RESOURCES

Listed below are links to few popular bridal web sites of interest. I have no commercial or financial connection with any of these companies; they are listed purely as a convenience for you.

FORUMS (UK)

Brides Wedding Forum	www.bridesweddingforum.co.uk/Forum/index
Hitched	www.hitched.co.uk/chat/forums
You & Your Wedding	www.youandyourwedding.co.uk
Wedding Chaos	www.weddingchaos.co.uk/wedding-forum
Wedding Forum	www.weddingforum.co.uk

FORUMS (USA)

Brides	www.brides.com/forums/index.jspa
Best Destination Wedding	www.bestdestinationwedding.com/forum

RETAIL SHOPS

Debenhams	www.johnlewis.com/Gifts/Wedding/Category.aspx
House of Fraser	www.houseoffraser.co.uk
John Lewis	www.debenhams.com/weddings

WEDDING FAYRES

All Wedding Fayres — www.allweddingfayres.co.uk

CJ Wedding Fayre (Wales) — www.cjweddingfayres.co.uk

Guides for brides — www.guidesforbrides.co.uk

National Wedding Show — www.nationalweddingshow.co.uk

Wedding Fayres (UK) — www.weddingfayresuk.co.uk

MAGAZINES

Brides Magazine — www.bridesmagazine.co.uk

You & Your Wedding — www.youandyourwedding.co.uk

Wedding Magazine — www.weddingmagazine.co.uk

Wedding Ideas Magazine — www.weddingideasmag.com

BEAUTY

Bobby Brown — www.bobbibrowncosmetics.com/home.tmpl

Clinique — www.clinique.co.uk

Elizabeth Arden — www.shop.elizabetharden.com/home/index.jsp

Kerastase — www.kerastase.co.uk/_en/_gb/home/index.aspx

Lancome — www.lancome.co.uk/_en/_gb

Revlon — www.revlon.com/#/2

Shiseido — www.shiseido.com/index.htm

DRESSES

ABC Weddings — www.abcweddingdresses.co.uk
Browns Fashion — www.brownsfashion.com/cm/bridalhome.htm
Ian Stuart — www.ianstuart-bride.com
Maggie Sottero — www.maggiesottero.com
Sarah Jackson — www.sarahjacksondesigns.co.uk
Sassi Holford — www.sassiholford.com
Vera Wang — www.verawangonweddings.com/Default.aspx
Wedding Dresses UK — www.weddingdressplace.com
Wedding Elegance — www.weddingeleganceuk.co.uk

HAIR

Bridal Hair by Helen — www.bridalhairbyhelen.co.uk
Style-Hair Magazine — www.style-hair-magazine.com/hair-style-photo.html
You & Your Wedding — www.youandyourwedding.co.uk/cat/Hair

SHOES

Christian Louboutin — www.christianlouboutin.com
Gina — www.jimmychoo.com
Jimmy Choo — www.gina.com
Rainbow Club — www.rainbowclub.co.uk

FLOWERS

Angel Flowers   www.angel-flowers.co.uk

Blooming Linda   www.bloominglinda.co.uk

Cottage Flowers   www.cottageflowersandmore.co.uk

WEDDING PLANNERS

Weddings by Claire   www.weddingsbyclaire.co.uk

Essentially You   www.essentially-you.net

Supreme Luxury Wedding   www.supremeluxuryweddings.com/index.html

Wedding Wonders   www.wedding-wonders.com

BUILD YOUR OWN WEDDING WEBSITE

Free, and paid-for, wedding sites to record your total wedding experience and share with your family and friends online.

UK

www.momentville.com

www.simplywedded.co.uk

www.weddingpath.co.uk

US

www.brides.com/myweddingplanner/new

www.ewedding.com

www.thebridalbell.com/index.html

ABOUT THE AUTHOR

Helen grew up in Launceston, Cornwall where she gained a hairdressing apprenticeship, straight from college. Helen's speciality in bridal hair styling is based on her early salon training when long hair styles were popular. With over 30 years hairdressing experience, her qualified expertise extends to all hair types and aspects of hair styling – cutting, colouring, perming, highlights and, of course, advice.

After taking a few years off to raise a family of six children and help her husband run two businesses, Helen started hairdressing again by chance. A casual conversation with a local florist found Helen helping a bride at the last minute because her hairdresser had let her down. It involved the styling of her long hair on location, in her hotel room. The bride was delighted. As a result, word spread and more brides followed. Demand from local brides grew steadily and Helen soon found herself in a new business.

Helen has now been involved in personal bridal hair styling for 6 years. She regularly attends wedding fayres, giving demonstrations and styling the models for the catwalk. Helen is passionate about her work and thoroughly enjoys what she does: providing a dedicated service that helps her clients to feel and look fantastic on their wedding day.

Her overriding priority is to make her clients look beautiful and feel fantastic on their very special day. Apart from operating her own successful bridal hairdressing business, Helen now advises other hair stylists. She operates regular hair workshops for salon stylists; teaching them bridal styling techniques and long-hair skills.

BRIDAL HAIR *by* Helen

Helen is glad to receive feedback from readers and happy to answer any enquiries for bridal hair trials, workshop requests or exhibition demonstrations.

Please contact Helen through her website:

www.bridalhairbyhelen.co.uk

Notes
THINGS TO DO

Use this page to jot down any notes or reminders.

TASKS TO ORGANISE/COMPLETE ✓